IMPROVISATIONAL ARGUMENTS

POEMS BY

ANNA FAKTOROVICH

Fomite

BURLINGTON, VERMONT

Fomite

58 Peru Street

Burlington, VT 05401

www.fomitepress.com

Book design by Anna Faktorovich

Copyrights © 2011 by Anna Faktorovich

All rights reserved. No part of this book may be reproduced in any form or by any electronic or mechanical means, including information storage and retrieval systems, without permission in writing from Anna Faktorovich. Writers are welcome to quote brief passages in their critical studies, as American copyrights law dictates.

The cover image, "Fire Dimension," by Alex Aleksandrovich, is used under the Creative Commons public domain license.

Published in 2011 by Fomite

Improvisational Arguments

Anna Faktorovich—1st edition.

ISBN-13: 978-0-9832063-6-1

ISBN-10: 0983206368

Library of Congress Control Number: 2011914672

My mistress' eyes are nothing like the sun;
Coral is far more red than her lips' red;
If snow be white, why then her breasts are dun;
If hairs be wires, black wires grow on her head.

—WILLIAM SHAKESPEARE,
Segment of Sonnet 130

TABLE OF CONTENTS

POETIC THEORY: EPITHETS   9

PART I: TRAVELS   13

Cross-Country Driving	15
On the Eighteenth Hour	16
Skating to the Lake	18
Nashville	19
Square Dancing	20
Israeli Fever	21
Rabbi Rape	22
Venetian Music	24
Roman Ruins	25
Ballet	26
Should I Buy a Car or a Plane?	27
The Giant Gymnasium	28
Truro Beach	29
Wyoming	30
The Rodeo Hotel	31
Mountainside Mining	32
The Las Vegas Drummer	33
Washington D.C.	34
Charleston	35
The Florida Keys	36
Bahamas Cruise	37
Montreal Music Festival	38
A Night in a Los Angeles Barn Shelter	39
A Night in a Los Angeles JW Marriot Hotel	40
New Orleans after the Flood	41

A Trip through America   43
Mark Twain's House   46

PART II: FANTASY   47

Metaphysics   49
If There Were No Rules in Magic   50
Alien Visitor   51
The Vampire   52
Unicorn   53
Mermaid   54
Lilith   55
Centaur   56
Cyclops   57
My Friends   58
Your Imaginary Friends   59
Jade, the Magician   60
Wise Sayings from 498,062 AD   62
Witch's Garden   63
Gnome Infestation   66
The Bat Man   68
My Pet Sloth   71
Capitalist Farm   72
Fantasy Island   73
How to End World Hunger   74
The Robotic Maid   75
The Resurrection of Don Quixote   76
Pan's Portrait   77
An Average Day for a Pirate   78
A Highland Legend   80
Vestri's Confession   82

PART III: WORK AND ART   83

Managing a Porn Star   85
Rock Star's Double   86
Reading Poetry at Open-Mic Night in Columbia   87
The Heckler: Or, Stand-Up Comedy   88
To Tell a Poem   89
Improvisational Arguments   90
Communal Script Writing   91
The Slush Pile   92

PART IV: POLITICS   93

Campaigning for the Presidency   95
A Petition for Online Voting   96
Revolution   97
A Jacobite Rebellion   98
Do We Need a President?   99
Debt Ceiling   100
The Queen Visits Ireland   101
Billion Dollar Thefts of Iraqi Funds   102
The First Decade of the Iraq War   103
Mandatory Execution of Gang Members   104
Taxes   105
Faculty Are Managers in Ohio   106
An Online Education   107
If I Had a Robot Assistant   108
School vs. Town Elections   109
No More Snow in Moscow   110
Graduate Student Unions   111
Why Is There a Monarchy in England?   112
Why Is Gas the Popular Fuel?   113
Deepwater Horizon   114

"Most Presidents Have Ignored the War Powers Act"	115
Should We Sing "Barney" during Shootings?	116
How Much Does a Senate Seat Cost?	117
PART V: PETITIONS AGAINST MARRIAGE	119
A Borrowed Lover	121
He Looks Down	122
Confused Youth	124
Katya	126
Wild Woman	127
The Resurrection of the Rose	128
I Need a Man	129
Can I Go Upstairs to the Girls' Apartment?	130
The Wind	131
Massage	132
An Argument for the Illegalization of Marriage	133
The Guy with No Car	134
Skater after the Crash	135
The Guy Who Stares	136
Politics and Love	137
Prom with M.I.T.	138
The Last Kiss	139
Captured Grasshopper	140
Spring and Beauty	141
Associations	142

Poetic Theory: Epithets

Poetry can defy its definition by refusing to rhyme, and not working on a rhythm.

Prose poetry is neither a contradiction nor a paradox.

Poetry can be short or long, it can be punctuated or de-capitalized.

Poetry is written to tell an extremely short story that cannot be told in paragraphs of prose.

Poetry can paint beautiful pictures, or it can paint in darker, distorted colors.

Poetry can be political or apolitical.

Poetry should be clear, logical and readable, so that students and pleasure-seekers can understand it.

Poetry should be complex and multi-dimensional, so that it can offer something new when it is read a second time.

Poetry is written to be shared with the public. It is not a private diary.

A lot of the things said in poetry are lies, while other things are sincere truths.

We should not believe poets when they write about metamorphosis of trees.

We should believe poets when they write about the metamorphosis of people.

We do not live in the days when readers have the patience for epic poetry.

So we string together a hundred short poems, and call them collections.

All teachers of poetry should write poetry to show that they share a love for the craft.

All poets should teach poetry to share the craft they love with their students.

PART I

TRAVELS

Cross-Country Driving

A migration today is nothing like it was
In the times of *The Grapes of Wrath*.
A forty-five hour car-drive and you are in L. A.
Four days when the country flies by you,
When you struggle with your engine,
Up over the Pennsylvania highlands,
Over the Appalachian Mountains,
To the plains of Kentucky and Missouri,
Through prairies, steppes, moors, and marshes,
To the deserts of Colorado, Utah and Nevada,
Where the sand goes from yellow to red and back,
Where you drive through sand dunes
And Rocky Mountains,
And suddenly emerge
High on the Hollywood hills,
And a moment later, you are driving
By the Pacific Ocean.

On the Eighteenth Hour

An average set of tires can handle
Fifty thousand miles.
I can drive for eighteen hours
Before I need sleep.
My car is an old Toyota,
With a dented body, that drags wind,
As it struggles around the bruised
Highways and byways,
To a conference,
Then back home,
To teach next morning.
I grab the wheel and watch
The broken line on the left of the windshield.
And those repeating rectangles
Turn into white and yellow sheep,
Jumping by the side of my car,
Suggesting soft wool and sleep.
I stop for gas, coffee and a sandwich,
Taking them to-go.
When it gets dark, I feel a swelling,
As I get balloon feet,
And the speedometer pushes
Five miles over the limit,
And I watch it, careful not to go to ten,
To avoid a ticket.
So, after a paced start, I'm going faster,
Hoping to win
Six hours of sleep before
My cell's alarm clock wakes me.
The highway feels like a race track,

And the other cars are
Speeding by me, tailgating,
Cutting me off, beeping.
If I felt some road rage,
It would wake me,
But I don't.
I just watch them squeal and beep and drive by.
I stay at the limit, and signal my turns,
Steadily progressing.
And then the GPS tells me
To take my last turn,
And I roll down my old street.
I'm in my driveway.
Turn off the ignition.
Close my eyes.
"Another driving goal met."

Skating to the Lake

The apartment complex is noisy, and dirty,
So I put on a pair of black inline skates,
And roll carefully down the narrow pathway
To the wider sidewalk that leads to the lake.

The summer heat is easing as the sun sets.
The after-work traffic thins into clear streets.
I pick up speed, past the park and playground,
Over the bumps of the broken pavement.

Until I'm off the main road, on a side street,
Gliding downhill in the tucked position,
Possibly breaking the twenty-five speed limit.
I stretch my back, stand tall at the drop's end.

I push off near the hill's bottom to gain speed.
The climb up is hard; I push for every inch.
I breathe heavily and sweat until the next crest.
I jump and dance in half-loops on the slide.

In Brooklyn, I frequently saw tight packs
Of skaters, who went down the center of the street,
Their long, soft locks waving in the wind in unison.
But, they were all male, and rejected female interns.

There is a circling pack of them, chatting together.
I go by, trying to focus on the road, and on my speed.
I'm at my lake, spinning on the pavement by the docks.
I spread my arms and feel as free as a flying eagle.

Nashville

Nashville is a ghostly vibrant country city,
Where half-a-dozen street singers perform
At night on the Walk of Fame, hitting the bricks,
While behind them wealthy tourists eat haute cuisine.
Five million hotel rooms are sold in a year in Nashville.
Five billion dollars are made in a year on tourism.
But they walk by when you stretch your hand for a dime.
And when you drive two miles from the center,
You see closed shops, graffiti, and bars of those
Whose dreams of singing were crushed
At one of the nightclubs, where only the youthful win.

Square Dancing

Quilts were scattered without symmetry
Over the spacious walls of the Charleston,
West Virginia Capitol Building's reception area.
Quilts lined the background of the main theater,
Where the ceiling supported two giant abstract balls
Made out of crossed wires, crystals and light bulbs.
Five award flags hanged on the same wall.
Below those sat four musicians.
A lone woman was playing a tambourine.
Three male fiddlers were busy adjusting
Their strings and horsehair.
The only exceptions to the informal t-shirts
Of the audience, were the performers,
Spotlessly arranged in uniforms,
With smiles playing on their
Exquisitely made-up features.

Israeli Fever

The twelve-hour non-stop flight gave me a fever
By the time we arrived from New York in Ben Gurion.
But it was a group Birthright tour and I continued,
Thinking it might be just the summer Israeli heat.

We did not go to the Mediterranean Sea spas,
Nor did I swim in the thick pudding of the Dead Sea.
I did not listen to the Israeli Tel Aviv orchestra,
And I didn't go to the world-famous theaters.

It was 2002 and the peak of a terrorist conflict,
And we marched through the desert and through
The Gaza Strip, the contested war-torn segment
With a dozen soldiers with rifles over-shoulders.

We walked like Jacob when he first settled in Canaan,
Or like Moses, as he took the Jews out of Egypt,
Or like the first Jews that returned to the Holy Land,
Over sand, and rock, up mountains, in a fever.

We searched through the *Masada*, [מצדה] taking a cable car
To the top of a plateau, high enough to see Jordan.
We looked through the ruins like anthropologists,
Cataloging the Dovecote and the sandy Thermal baths.

From the ruins of the rebel dwellings, we marched
To the Wall of Tears and the Dome of the Rock.
And leaving a wish in the Wall, I had a bite of the
Bitter *hummus* [חומוס] and *falafel* [פלאפל] and cried through the fever.

Rabbi Rape

The news reports that priests frequently rape boys.
But I had never heard of a rabbi doing it
Until I had a fever on a Birthright trip.
I was dragged through the desert and ruins,
And caught a fever, and couldn't sleep
On a floor mat on the floor of a Bedouin tent.
So, I asked the counselor for advice,
And she directed me to the hotel-structure,
Visible from the open, crowded tents.
I could barely stand, and the sky span above.
I stumbled to the hotel and saw the
Rabbi standing in an open doorway.
The counselor called somebody before
Telling me where to go, so I assumed
That he was expecting me, and he was.
He stepped towards me as if to embrace me.
"I have a fever," I exclaimed.
"I was told I could rest in this… room."
He drew closer, and I stepped back,
Until he put his hand on my back,
And leaned in, as if for a caress.
I screamed "Rape!" and the Bedouins
Ran out of their rooms and asked what was wrong.
The counselor also heard, and ran up.
They met to discuss my fate, as I sat in a fever
Under a dry tree on the cold sand.
Then, they called me in, and the counselor
Told me that I had to go back home,
And had to pay for my trip.
I explained what happened,

But they covered up my protests,
And protected the rabbi,
Just like the Papacy has protected its priests.

Venetian Music

Venice is the city that bred Giacomo Casanova,
And it deserves the title of the Floating City,
As romance is best bred afloat on water in gondolas,
And love blooms better on a hundred tiny bridges.

"Grazie mille," you say to the bowtie waiter at *Caffe Florian*,
As you sit on a white chair outside and listen to the
Violins, flutes and pianos of the small classical band,
And eat a bite of the *tiramisu*, after a large *pasta di gamberetti*.

And then you stroll by the *Grand Canal* to the *Piazza San Marco*,
Inspecting the acid rain green streaks on the Gothic architecture,
And look across the sparkling water at the *San Giogrio Island*,
And you sit back down at another café and watch the dancers.

And you can hear every note ringing against the strings
Because there are no cars or bikes allowed in Venice,
So you take a motorboat and watch the outlines of the island,
As others exit, you stay for all the stops, and understand…

How while Casanova had a thousand love affairs here,
Renaissance painters climbed the stairs and painted
Ceilings with beautiful people, working into the night,
Creating the Gothic bridges that others fall in love on.

Roman Ruins

To see the full panorama,
Go to the Palatinno of Roma,
Under the blazing sun, where your hat
Won't stop the burning sweat.
Sit on top of the red ruins
And watch the field of yellow grass,
Empty and sparkling with glass.
Look at the marvelous white domes in the distance
And at the cars roaring by below
And at the busy bundle of houses—
Filling the gaps between the ruins and cars.
The trees remain, holding their ground—
Few, but as green as ever.
Stare at it for a moment.
Breathe in the stench and the hay.
Blood flows through this city, filled with angels.
If you get lost in the mazes, don't yell.
They might think you an odd blackbird—
Like those flying above that give the only shadows—
Garrulously invading your private space.

Ballet

Freelance writers usually write on assignments,
But occasionally I picked my own feature topics,
Like the time I did a piece on the Boston Ballet,
Buying my own student ticket at a discount price.

I saw two different shows of the same Swan Lake
On consecutive nights, the choreography changed,
The costumes changed, and the dancers changed,
Even the orchestra played different rhythms and melodies.

The dancers' lines were straight and their jumps fierce.
They swam across the floor in their hard boxed shoes,
Waving their red and white tutus and graceful fingers,
Stretching their muscular inner thighs in black tights.

After the show, an administrator led me backstage,
And pointed out Director Mikko Nissinen, still busy,
Speaking formally with the families of the company,
As a few dancers rehearsed pliés, as in a Degas sketch.

I approached the principle dancer, Misa Kuranaga, a tall Japanese girl,
And she invited me to come with her and her dance partner
To a restaurant and we chatted about the pointe shoes…
But, I never published the piece—the paper didn't want positive reviews.

Should I Buy a Car or a Plane?

Next year, I will final have enough money saved.
I was going to buy a new car, just out of the factory.
But, living in Edinboro, a city in the middle of nowhere
Has made me wonder if I need a car or a plane.

I found a nineteen-seventy Grumman Yankee Clipper
That's done three thousand miles since nineteen seventy,
It carries twenty-four gallons and costs seventeen thousand,
And can take me to Florida or California twice faster than a car.

I would fly into isolated islands, to Hawaii, to Alaska,
And there would be no traffic, except near the landing,
And there would be no rude passengers, and no delayed flights,
And I would see all around, instead of through a narrow window.

But then I wonder if it's safe, and I wonder why it was flown
For only a few thousand miles in its forty years in operation,
When my ten-year car has two-hundred thousand on it,
And I wonder about parking, and customs, and flight lessons.

What do other professors spend their money on?
Vacation homes? Mortgages? Kids? Sports cars? Boats?
Are there millionaires out there who don't buy a plane?
I'm not sure if I'll buy a plane, but if I do, I'm going to Hawaii.

The Giant Gymnasium

I suspect that people who become Olympic athletes
Started training in fantastical upscale gyms
With bikes and rowing machines with game displays
And TV screens, and perfect traction.

The first time I started exercising regularly
Was in one of these gyms at USC,
With a grand view from wall-length windows,
With a sauna, Jacuzzi, and an Olympic pool.

I tried exercising in big gyms after it,
And in small private gyms, with ten machines.
But I had to buy my own rower and bike
Because there was something magical about that giant gym.

Truro Beach

The beaches are better in Massachusetts not because
They are cleaner, or cheaper, or sandier, or longer,
But because the winter is longer than in the south,
And when the summer comes, the beaches are heavenly.

They have nude beaches, isolated and popular beaches.
But my favorite beach has always been in Truro,
Where the hostel is, and only three other houses,
And I walk for miles along the water, nearly alone.

Sometimes surfers come there, at other times, locals,
So, I wander off into the raspberry forest, uphill,
Or into the butterfly-infested dunes, or watch the waves
From the rocks that are piled high, and stretch far into the sea.

The waves crash against the rocks, as the sun sets,
 And I sit and smell the sun's scent lingering on my arm,
And watch the seagulls, and the baby birds running on the sand,
And I watch the stars as they appear, and have a moment to relax.

Wyoming

There is a house in Wyoming
With a wide corroded terrace,
Overlooking a large goat farm.
On its side there is construction,
For a new bigger house.
There is a brook running along the farm,
There are sandy hills
In the near distance,
And the grass is thin
Because it is a northern desert.
Beyond the hills,
There is endless free space,
And no houses or roads
For miles in most directions.

The Rodeo Hotel

On a byway in the Wild West,
There is a small hotel,
Where travelers stop, when they
Run out of gas, or fall asleep
From the repeating farms,
Wheat tours, and grass.
And across from the hotel
There is a rodeo space,
With thick wooden posts,
And a small stage with hanging seats.
Snow and rain falls
On this abandoned rodeo
All year, until June,
When the region's cowboys
Gather and show their skills,
And ride the horses and bulls,
And the neighboring country folk
Sit in the stands and cheer
And stay at the old Rodeo Hotel.

Mountainside Mining

The machines scrape stone from the sides
Of mountains in West Virginia, stripping the scene.
Then, these stone slabs are transported to
Stone yards for shaping, sanding, cutting and polishing,
Until they are turned into square chunks of stone,
And arranged in rows, with yellow lines on the
Pavement separating the isles of stone.
They sparkle in a thousand stone colors:
Brown, white with streaks, mixes,
Wood-like circles in the granite, white marble,
Red and yellow annex, gold limestone,
And blue glass with white dots.
The yard is next to a river because they used to
Float the stone in barges, and later by steamboat.
Across the river, there is an apartment complex
That probably doesn't advertise the view of the yard.
When an order comes in, an overhead crane
Rolls to the desired slab, lifts it and carries it
To the opened garage entrance,
And it is hauled into a truck and shipped
To a luxurious dining room as a counter.

The Las Vegas Drummer

He went to Las Vegas for the gambling,
And stayed to drum for the belly dancers,
Who danced with their stomachs and
Flexed their arms and legs to his rhythm.

He imagined that he was in Arabian Nights,
Playing a beat to make the snakes move
In the direction that he pleased, making them
Slither in their leathery skin across the dance floor.

At night he would drive down Fremont Street,
Imagining the city as a Christmas tree from above,
Parking and walking into the Fitzgeralds and
Touching the machines, but keeping his coins.

During the day, he drove out of the city,
Through dry mountains in subtropical heat,
Under a cloudless sky, and nearly fainted,
In that arid basin of the desert's floor.

His eyes squinted and he heard the rhythm of the past,
Mexican colorful dresses flying before the War,
Then the dust of a railroad and then a mining town,
And the recent housing boom and recession bust.

He came back home and wrote the lyrics down,
But played only the beat for the belly dancers.

Washington D.C.

I visited D.C. to research Abolitionist women
In the archives of the Library of Congress.
I stayed in a hostel because I also went to
Philadelphia and Durham, on a tight budget.

I arrived in the evening and visited the
South West quadrant at sunset, walking down
A path along the mighty Potomac River,
Under the grand oaks, as if the city disappeared.

Next morning, I drove into city center,
Built on a special charter to avoid another Mutiny,
Re-built after fires, and decades of rough usage,
And parked for a twenty at the Union Station.

I walked to the Library through the city
That saw many assassinations, wars, and sieges,
Along the Reflecting Pool that was stormed by a sea
During the great March on Washington.

I remembered visiting the renovated split Congress,
The House Chamber on one end, on the other the Senate.
And looking up the National Gallery's tall glass ceiling,
Walking over the marble bridge across the wide central space.

But, now, walking directly into the Library
And reading scrolls, as if there were no wonders outside.

Charleston

Why do most people live in the cold North,
When in the warm south, in Charleston,
Blooms society, culture, and art as if nourished
By the climate, and by the calm surrounding sea.
I skate down King Street at night, staring at
The mansions built side-by-side like in Manhattan,
And glance inside at the interior gardens,
And through the windows at the oak and marble,
And at the sports cars that don't fit into the garages.
I swing on the double-seated swings at the bay,
Watching the seagulls that walk nearby
Because there are only a few people on the walkway.
I notice a dolphin jumping out of the water,
And watch the sun playing on the clean waves.
And a horse-drawn carriage trots down the cobwebs,
And musicians play in the street in this warm Paradise.

The Florida Keys

Venice was built with hundreds of bridges.
But there is only one bridge-overseas-highway,
Famous for its Seven Mile Bridge,
Stretching between thousands of islands in the Keys.
The road divides the Atlantic from the Gulf,
And you drive down it with miles and miles
Of pristine blue water on both sides of the car.
When I reach an island, I see tropical palms,
And in the distance, empty sandy beaches,
With a few private boats, sailing or docked.
If only the short-lived Conch Republic survived,
And this odd otherworldly space was its own country.

Bahamas Cruise

The Bahamas are much closer to the U.S.,
But like Cuba, its near-neighbor they are independent,
Unlike Hawaii, which, while it is much further,
Stranded, in isolation, in the middle of the ocean,
Was recently declared one of the United States.
The Bahamas stand on islands, corals and rocks,
And house fewer people than the Keyes,
And the populace is poor, and lives in cardboard,
Clay and plastic sheds, only ten-feet long.
Bahamas, and not U.S., should celebrate
Columbus Day, as he landed there,
And probably would not have stayed,
If, instead, he landed in New England in the winter.
But it was not a part of the initial "Independence"
Deal with the United Kingdom, and had to fight
For its own rights a century later, and now
I'm a tourist sailing in on a cruise ship, and
Look at the magnificent steep rocks, behind the
Ship-parking lot of the Nassau Harbor.

Montreal Music Festival

The summer heat drove me north,
And soon I was at a café in Montreal.
I noticed a crowd and followed them to the
Festival International de Jazz de Montréal.
I watched, hypnotized, a string of free tunes.
Guitarists with dreadlocks rocked.
A beautiful pianist in a skirt and a tall afro
Was accompanied by a percussionist quartet
In rimmed black hats and suites.
On a different stage a gracious French woman,
With short, black, round hair, extensive eyelashes
And blue eye shadows, was playing on the Soul.
Inside a restaurant, a soloist sang in French and English
To a post-modern improvisational drum-jazz,
Shaking his contemporary-art hair, jelled to stay-on-end.
For once, I did not feel foreign as I stood among
Traveling artists from Cuba, America, France and Africa,
Battling for the title of the best jazz performance in the world.

A Night in a Los Angeles Barn Shelter

"Not enough room to swing a cat!"
My neighbor said.
As she insisted on throwing her coat
At me as I slept.

The room was full with five-hundred souls.
The sheets smelled
Like they were used by them all.
I tried to ignore the mold.

The ladies screamed past one o'clock.
They opened stalls
While I was there, as if they couldn't see
Through the short doors.

There was no dinner left by eight,
When I arrived after
A day of interviewing through the recession
And writing nights.

Can it be legal to cram five-hundred into a barn?
Why are there twenty employees, but dirty stalls?
Why don't they help when I say, "I'm harassed?"
I leave at one, and sleep in my car till dawn.

A Night in a Los Angeles JW Marriot Hotel

A year later, I see the city from a different view,
From the top floor of JW Marriot, the location for the *Inception*.
Three maids rustle sheets down the long hallway.
There isn't a speck of dust, only a light perfume.
The shower door is clear,
And my shampoo is the size of a thumb.
I wash my hair after the long flight,
And it smells like pine.

I invite a co-worker for a business meeting.
We sit on the red, curved, just-soft-enough
Couch—discussing academics, editing,
Sales, graduate school, conferences…
I glance out of the window—
At the sea, at the skyline.
I tell him that I have to finish some work.
He leaves politely.
And I sit at the desk and edit my presentation,
And glance outside.

New Orleans after the Flood

Right after the semester starts,
I hear the news—
New Orleans was flooded during Katrina.
I try to think about the Charleston beaches,
But I can't help checking how far it is.

How does eighty-one billion dollars
In property damages look?
As if only a moment later, I arrive, and see
Highway signs torn down,
Half of a room and a quarter of a floor
Scattered along the beach,
A gas station with its columns knocked down.

I eat in a restaurant,
Where they don't have chocolate,
And other rudiments of good eatery.
The devastation is at its worst in the French Quarter,
Where history is ruined, and lying wasted.

I read Fanny Trollope's description of the magic
Of the New Orleans levee system centuries ago.
She wondered at how man-made inventions
Kept back the tides of the entire sea,
That took four months to cross.

I roam the damaged streets, torn by Nature,

But I don't see a single brick-layer.
No government contractors or police offers.
There is no response, no re-building,
No assistance for the homeless,
Drug-addicts, and others in the poor district.
A bearded man asks me to help,
And I clean bricks from his yard.

A Trip through America

Highway signs bended, tossed
Into the shrubbery.
Roofs without shingles cover the ruins.
The white sand littered with bricks,
Branches, foundations.
A boy is selling chips to buy a ticket away,
Fifty cents for directions to the next beach,
The next soul-torment,
Away from the four cars under a gas station roof,
Where his dead parents used to work.

A waif is sleeping in his van,
Next to his locked-down home.
"You come to witness the destruction?
"The milking cow is dead,
"Sin was washed away by da water."
At night, he looks through his windshield,
At a sheet of constellations above,
At the white bricks of a new house,
And remembers the old one that flew away.
He wishes he could move into a trailer,
Parked for sewage in a richer driveway.
Awakening, he sees tombstones in the yards
And dozens of starving ghosts floating by,
Hears the rustling leaves of a barren palm tree.
"This City is built too low, a Babel built backwards,
"Down into a dead womb."

A film-crew's eating breakfast at "Mother's,"
Interacting with crazy locals.
"My movie this... My movie that..."
"Six films shooting at Orleans..."
Shooting the survivors.
Point the camera there!

Four crying, starving children!

A dead dog in the street!
It smells!
Where are the garbage trucks?
Too much garbage to throw away.
Can't throw away a city.

Ten hours North-West,
To the President's home state,
To a dead cypress lake.
Trees standing stripped and gray in the still water.
A waitress sits on the dock.
She's not a waitress no more,
For saying the place was gonna get sold.
Will get evicted tomorrow.
Husband beat her that morning.
Sitting, looking for a boat-buyer.
"Good deal. I'll let it go for a thousand today."
It's a good buying day
When the country's this low,
Lower than worms,
Low like my heart,
Sunk into my empty womb,
Starving for affection.

Wander barefoot on a side-street.
The earth is covered with four-leaf clovers,
And cow feces.
Two men in a truck stop,
"Is your car broken down?"
"No Sir. I'm all right."
Let me hug this tree here,
This one that's blooming,
This strong tree,
Full of life in the middle of a broken America.
Am I crazier than you to hug a tree,
While you sit in your truck?
Leave me alone with my peaceful Lover.

Mark Twain's House

While some say that a writer only needs
A Room of One's Own to create art,
Mark Twain clearly needed a nineteen-room
Mansion in Connecticut, and not a room in
Missouri in a family home in a small country-town.
But it started with a small room-house
Outside of his wife's sister's mansion,
And soon ballooned into a project.
He insisted on the fancy decorations,
And on the fine furniture, and long chimneys.
He needed a family with three daughters,
To critique his drafts over the dinner table.
Only when he was sitting on a gilded chair
In a Library with hundreds of books could he
Look with detachment on his days in Missouri
And write about Finn and Sawyer,
About the Prince and the Pauper,
As if poverty was a distant concept that
He could describe and catalogue from the
Heights of his third-story carved window.

PART II

FANTASY

Metaphysics

The trouble with metaphysics is that it's a misnomer.
We should blame Aristotle's editor, Andronicus of Rhodes.
He explained that Aristotle's book came "after" *Physics*.
Or should we blame translators who said it was "beyond?"
Are Aristotle's *Poetics* and *Rhetoric* inferior to physics?
Do philosophers study spirits and non-concrete things?
Should science be enough to answer if we exist?
Should philosophy skip over metaphysics as superficial?
No, Aristotle did not think his philosophy was physical.
Philosophy is the science of studying hypothesis and
Literary generic rules, and the order of proper thought.
Let's abandon metaphysics, and let's study philosophy.

If There Were No Rules in Magic

If there were no rules in magic, the protagonist witch
Could do anything she'd imagine, without bounds.
She would fly without a broom, or appear anywhere,
She would make castles and diamonds with her thoughts.
She would not need to wave a wand or utter incantations.
She would never die, and could live without air and food.
She wouldn't have any enemies because she'd have everything,
And would never have to battle for any wish or whim.
She could not be good or evil because she would
Write the book of what is good and what is evil,
And would not be subordinate to any man or god,
And would own the world one day, and give it away the next.
But without the rules of magic, she would have a very short story.

Alien Visitor

I was lying in bed, about to fall asleep, when I heard a knock
On my window, and opened it to find an alien staring at me.
He was surprisingly cute, with a broad pink chest,
And big black eyes, and thin hands and legs, with fancy shoes.
He was a bit shorter than me, and stared up at me with his
Giant eyes for a long moment, until I asked him,
"Are you lost?" He was quiet for a while, and then replied,
"My interplanetary translator is a bit slow, and yes, I am.
"I hoped to land a few solar systems over, but got drunk,
"And landed here instead. Do you have any… beer?"
"Beer? You have beer on your planet?" "Yep."
I let him in through my large window and he sat in the kitchen.
I gave him a beer, and had one myself.
He started to fall asleep in the sitting position, whistling with his ears,
But I led him to my couch and he passed out until morning,
When he awoke, he thanked me, climbed out, and flew home.

The Vampire

"So, you would like to know what it is like
"To live as a vampire, well it's not great.
"I developed vampirism early in life,
"And it meant that I could never eat
"Meat, or milk, or even wine again.
"If I try, I vomit, and can't swallow it.
"In the movies, the vampires eat human blood.
"But, in reality I'd get arrested that same night.
"I can't fly, and I can't hear thoughts,
"And my health is weak, and I'll probably
"Croak before I turn fifty, as all the books say
"That people must eat a balanced meal,
"And blood does not have the nourishment
"To give a man health."
Thus spoke the thin, frail vampire,
Sitting across from me, and I wrapped up
The interview, and left the scene,
As the vampire reeked like dried blood,
And had stains from the pigs on his
Soiled scarf.

Unicorn

It was a sunny day, and I was riding my beige horse,
Across the toll grass on my farm, its tail flapping,
In the bright sun, under the thick green canopy.
And suddenly I saw a small horn growing
From its forehead, and I thought it was a trick of the sun,
But it was soon ten-inches long, and sparkled like a diamond.
I reached out and touched the edge, and felt
The horse start galloping, and then it made a leap
Over the fence and up into the cumulus clouds,
And when I thought we would fall, it grew wings,
And we flew high enough to see the whole state,
And then returned to my farm, and the horn and wings disappeared,
Then I was back at my window, across the street
From the beige horse on the tall-grassed farm.

Mermaid

I was swimming in the sea, jumping over a wave,
When I looked down and saw a scaly tale.
I trembled, briefly distressed, but then dived in,
And I could feel my chest breathe inside the wave,
So I pushed down into the depth, and further away.
The bottom of the sea was rich with corals and shells,
And I swam deeper until I saw squids and lanternfish,
And forests of seaweed, and castles of sand.
I was weightless and sped through the water
Like I was a part of the sea, then suddenly
I blinked and opened my eyes, and was back
On the sand, burned around the eyes.

Lilith

Lilith had a disagreement with Adam.
They were discussing her right to speak.
"Good morning," Lilith said, when they woke.
"You can't speak, you are a woman," Adam grumbled.
Lilith was silent for a while, as there was
Nobody to talk to in the Garden but Adam.
And Adam was also silent, and couldn't talk.
Next morning, when Lilith woke up, she felt
Adam on top of her, trying to have intercourse,
And she pushed him away with her strong legs,
And he screamed that she was created for him,
And she did not answer, but called God,
And asked for a termination of her marriage contract,
And God made Eve, and Lilith was free.

Centaur

A brook behind the butcher's shop ran whisht.
The silence drowned the town's gagged deafness.
A centaur broke through the branches and dashed
At a blond, barefooted shopkeeper in a nightdress.
A yell of pain brought the town's citizens out.
The beast stumped his hoofs and gave a horned pout.
"Where can a horse-man go to procreate today?!
"My father, Centaurus, mated with mares for horseplay.
"But, today grass-eaters are shunned like old boots."
The police chief stared, briefly aghast from shock,
Then raised his fire-lock and gave the beast a parting shot.
The barbarian galloped away, tearing bundles of roots.
He ran for hours without a stop, but finally fell,
"Why don't they put a saddle on me, for this is hell!"

Cyclops

A one-eyed giant was found in the basement
Of an abandoned leaf metal factory,
Making lightning bolts for Zeus's ascent,
Not knowing the God had long settled in Hawaii,
But forgot to tell the Cyclops about this.
He was arrested because his passport said, "Greece."
He was also charged with trespassing in long johns,
And for forging unlicensed explosive weapons.
There were many obstacles to the seizure.
There were no chains or ropes long enough for him.
No prison or jail could fit him.
They couldn't even stuff him in the largest sewer.
So he was asked to return to the factory
And keep himself busy for eternity.

My Friends

On the commode an elf with a whisker
Is purring, licking the last drop of soup.
Under the bed a gnome is enforcing order,
While sending dust flying to the roof.
A water spirit is bathing in the sink.
Apollo's crown is shining through the shades.
Three women are sitting in the kitchen,
Spinning, spinning, as brisk as spiders—
Skeptics say, "Their yarn's a fairy tale;"
Theorists, "It's a dance of golden threads."
Among this agitated, boisterous toil,
I wistfully stare, admiring my magical friends.
And, as I pace around my cabinet, I sigh—
My friends can't hug me, as I break and cry.

Your Imaginary Friends

Draw what you see.

Jade, the Magician

A long, red Chinese robe,
Joints curve gently, elegantly
Poking halls in paper, with her acrylic nails,
Pulling out colored handkerchiefs,
Bobbing her head like a doll,
A smile frozen on her red lips,
Hair pinned in a bun,
Serving magic, like tea,
In a performance meant for kings.
Down South, she's an Oriental puppet.

She throws up a sheet.
Drops it.

She's in a red, tight, slashed evening gown.
The music turns techno.
She starts to speak quickly,
Something Asian.
Stops.
"Yes."
The audience answers.
Her eyes laugh.
She switches to accent-less English.
She's American.
The most beautiful magic-trick of the night.
We stare.
But she looked Chinese.
She dressed Chinese.
She moved in Chinese.
Now, she walks like a nightclub dancer,
Invites two "grandpas" on stage,
And gropes their asses,
Lets them hug her tight,
Till her boobs are squeezed against them.
She makes bondage jokes.
The kids stare,
"Where did the nice Chinese lady go?"

Wise Sayings from 498,062 AD

"When the Hairballs are all gone, I'm gonna hunt the bugs. When I ain't got my gun, I ain't free." —Salaon

"Are there nails on your driveway? Don't check with your toes. Wear shoes." —Mazaduk

"A wife that makes jokes at dinner, makes her husband wash the dishes afterwards." —Saint-Fair

"I'm a mighty rebel.
"You're no-good foe.
"We'll give you hell,
"You'll leave our shore." —Rebel Rhyme

Witch's Garden

Gaia was sitting on a velvet throne,
In a silk green dress, painted
With tiny orange tulips,
Near a castle in France, looking out
At the bees sipping on the orange
Dandy lion-like elfworts.
She studied the circling lines of the
Green leaves and
The sepals of sage and vervain,
The red and yellow
Flowers and the heavy heads of the
Black-seeded poppies,
The giant yellow sun flowers,
Their stigmas pregnant with seeds,
The yellow, pink and
White clusters of yarrows,
The light purple clary sage,
The brown veins in the
Beige heads of the henbanes,
Rainbow-colored mushrooms,
And the pink, luxurious,
Long petals of the belladonnas,
Separated from each other by
Lines of elaborate, giant seashells.
A line of white, pinks, and crimson
Rose bushes hugged the castle's walls.

She listened as the strings of bells
Of the pink and light purple foxgloves
Rang, as their dew dropped
With a light touch of the wind.

The castle was on a cliff.
Looking to the right, Gaia could see
The black rocks at the edge
And the foam at the tips of
The sea's waves, as they calmly approached.

In the other direction, beyond the
Harvest of herbs for magic spells,
Were bushes cut in the shape of
Huntsmen, mermaids, and gnomes.
In the middle of the main path,
Water was purring as it spilled
Into each of the three cups
Of the marble water fountain.

Still further, a brook ran
At the edge of the field,
And just after it, a wall of
Tall oaks surrounded the garden,
So that no traveler might glance in.

Finally her gaze fell on the
Walkway that led to the stone gate,
Barely visible through the wall of
Blooming flowers and bushes.
She extinguished the tall
Candles that she burned for a ritual,
Spread her silky arms,
And flew up, until the garden
Looked like a spec at the edge
Of a limitless ocean.

Gnome Infestation

One day, I noticed that all of my five-hundred-year,
Tall English oaks had giant holes in their trunks.
The bark was peeling off, as if it was chewed on.
Their crowns were thinned and leaves turned brown.
Cracked chestnut-brown acorns littered the ground.
There were fewer insects in the bark than usual.
I didn't hear a woodpecker or any other beasts
That had long been visitors to that grove.
"It will take me fifty years to grow new oaks,"
I thought, and decided to investigate what happened.

Since there were no signs of life during the day,
I returned at night, walking softly to prevent
Warning the trespassers of my stealthy approach.
Even from a few feet into the forest, I noticed a glimmer.
As I walked further, it started to look like a candle.
My mouth dropped when I entered the oak grove.

There were candles in nearly every
Giant, enlarged hole in the oaks.
Yellow-orange lights could even be visible underground,
Through the dry, thick forty-feet-long roots.
Scrolls were left on the spreading branches,
As if somebody ran away in a hurry.
I tried to spot my foes through the
Darkness and the thick hugging fog.
But only made out chests with treasure.
I recovered from my fright and approached
One of the larger holes, and peered in.
I saw a gnome there with a long, white beard,
Chewing an open acorn in a carved oak seat.

I had a long chat with the gnomes and they
Explained that they moved into the oaks
In an attempt to build humanoid homes.
I countered that they were on my property,
But they insisted that they lived under those oaks
For several millenniums, so I gave up and
Planted apple trees closer to my house.

The Bat Man

I used to work as a zoologist
And my zoo once captured
A Mayan, Mexican bat man.

I studied his habits and appearance,
And decided that he belonged to the
Hairy-legged species of bats because
Of his hairy feet, chest and back,
And tall, nearly-black pointed ears.

He had an overdeveloped throat
That emitted ultrasonic sounds,
Which came back as echoes
So that he could detect objects at night.
But he had small poorly developed eyes,
Which he said were hereditary
In his family that lived in isolation.
I couldn't find eyeglasses strong enough.

The bones of his arms extend into
Additional small bones that formed wings
And his skin stretched out from
The meaty arms to the
Meatless edges of the wings.

At first I gave him steak and vegetables,
But he couldn't digest them.
So I switched to fruits.
But he asked for flower nectar,
Then for insects, and the blood of birds.

Sometimes I stayed after closing,
And entered his cage and sat with him.
He would flap down from the cage's roof,
And would wobble on his clawed-feet,
Shyly, over to my folding chair.
He would wait motionless for several minutes,
Nibbling and sucking on a rose.
Then, sneakily, as if just picking up another flower,
He would brush his rough finger tips
Over my fingers, stopping on their pillows.

From that tint of a touch, he'd progress to
Handling my open-sandal toes with his heels,
Impressing his fingers into my soft skin,
Moving, striking, stirring, agitating, shifting,
Raising, shaking, shifting, grabbing, swaying,
Making a kerfuffle out of my combed hair,
Curiously comparing my cold hands and hot forehead,
Reading the lines of my wrinkles like Braille,
Stopping to examine the cement-like, papier-mâché
Rough newspaper sheets of the skin on my neck,
Then, suddenly, melting, softly patting, tapping,
Caressing, and stroking my nose.
He exerted pressure on my skin,
Scratching it accidentally with his claws.

Months later, I was re-assigned and didn't know
How to say good bye to my shy bat man.
I sat with him that evening, and he could sense it,
Playing a game of touch-me-not,
As I nervously fingered the string of the cage.
Before I knew it, he took hold of the tips
Of my fingers and asked me if he was
Allowed to fly away, once I was gone.

My Pet Sloth

As a child, I ran away to South America
And lived on tree branches in the tropics.
I woke up one warm morning and discovered
A large sloth, with black highlights around the eyes,
Three thin claws on his paws, and long, wiry hair,
Lying behind me, hugging me around the shoulder.
I woke up when instead of scratching himself
He scratched me, lightly, and then yawned.
I gave a light scream, and the sloth opened his eyes.
"Shhh!" the sloth exclaimed and re-shut his eyes.
It turned out that there was a tribe of talking sloths
In that area and they befriended me until I moved north.
It was the most relaxing summer of my life,
As the tribe just ate, slept and scratched
Their backs against the trunks of palm trees.
I fit in perfectly well until I found an abandoned library,
And read a full collection of Tolstoy's novels.

Capitalist Farm

The animals on a capitalist farm
Are not like the ones in *Animal Farm*
Because the livestock does not rebel
Against the owners, but works
The same shifts as the farmers.
Capitalist farms are specialized.
So cows, chickens, horses and fowl don't mix.
On a dairy farm, five-hundred cows get dizzy,
As they spin on a rotating milking parlor.
A machine fastens onto the cow's breasts,
And sucks the milk out until it's thin,
Then another cow is suckled,
While the cows at the end of the circle
Eat grass or corn, as the owner can afford,
Until they are ready to give more milk.

Fantasy Island

When I made my first billion dollars,
I bought an island and started re-building
The natural tropical beauty into a private resort.
I began by adding a water park, a petting zoo,
A roller coaster, a massage and beauty parlor,
Then, a palace on the white sanded beach,
In a spot by the waterfalls, known for its
Daily rainbows and tropical gardens and
The outlying giant fern tree forest.
I even tamed the wild river
With my riverboat cruise trips.
I added a Jacuzzi on the nose of the ship,
With a view of the blue ocean and
Soft leather loveseats in the tropical motif
Stood, under a shade, around the pool.
I domesticated a group of exotic,
Giant, multi-colored, talking parrots,
And they sang pirate songs from their perches,
As I gazed at the purple and red skyline at sunset.

How to End World Hunger

While a billion people go hungry daily world-wide,
In Asia, and Africa, and also here in America,
There is a way to end all of that hunger if resources
Are directed to a proactive solution, instead of
Being lost in bureaucratic hassles and red rape.
The goals set by the World Food Summit a decade ago
Haven't been met; instead, hunger is on a rise.
The world produces enough food,
It just doesn't get to the poor who need it.
So, instead of shipping food to the hungry,
We should build programs like the Fantastic Food Plant
Engineered by the local scientists in India.
A single three-story building cooks enough
Food to make a hundred-thousand meals-a-day.
Twenty thousand of these dispersed around the globe,
Would end world hunger in the long-term.
Of course, they would have to add an automated
Farm that would grow rice, vegetables, beans, and wheat.
One out of seven people on earth go hungry.
But creating a factory run by the poor that produces
A hundred thousand meals-a-day is a bit too much
Like a return to nineteenth century industrialization
With its sweatshops, and child labor.
But shouldn't everyone who's hungry
Have a chance to make their own food?

The Robotic Maid

After scratching my knees trying to clean the attic,
I ordered a new service that became hip in the suburbs.
A robot rolled in on its one wheel to my door.
I watched from the couch as it cleaned my crib.
It began by polishing and wiping the glass, screens,
Tracks and frames of the round and wall-sized windows,
Then, scrubbed the newly painted walls and ceilings,
Polished all of the crystals and gold of the chandelier,
Took clothing out of the closets and wiped the wood,
Lifted the exercise equipment, and king beds
And vacuumed and cleaned the carpets under them,
Unhinged the cabinets in the kitchen, and cleaned out
The rodent and insect-inhabited wooden walkways,
Then used a high-tech heated power washing device to
Wash away leaves from rain gutters and sprinkler stains,
Finally sucking the dust out of the air ducts.
I thought it was cheap, until I saw the water and electric bills.

The Resurrection of Don Quixote

A wizard's spell went awry, as he was standing
Over the grave of the original Don Quixote,
So after the wizard wrapped his tools and left,
Quixote scratched his way out of his tomb.

The last thing he remembered was dying in bed,
But now he was as fresh and healthy as an ox.
He marched into a neighboring field and
Mounted a horse that reminded him of his mare.

He rode the mare into a motel and proposed
Marriage to the cleaning lady, smelling her bare toes.
Things went down-hill from there because
Attacking trucks isn't as safe as charging windmills.

Pan's Portrait

His long, curly hair was pulled up
Into a ponytail with a flowery vine.
His long goat-horns curled in a couple loops.
Above his chiseled jaw were long,
Hairy pointed ears with gold seashell earrings.
His chest and neck were broad and muscular.
His goat-legs were thin by the hoofs,
But thicker than most men on the thighs.
His hair sparkled in the morning sun,
As he had just taken a long bath in the pond.

An Average Day for a Pirate

Beardie awoke to the yell,
"Avast, up and smartly, our shift!"
He nearly fell out of his hammock, but regained balance,
And pulling on his breeches, waistcoat and cap,
Sprang away from the cluttered site of the
Twenty hammocks in the forecastle's berth,
Where seventy men slept in rotating shifts,
Onto the deck and to the stern,
Past the captain's quarters, and to his first duty,
Shifting the rudder plate to maneuver
The ship to the right, as the prior shift's sailing master
Was a lefty and always let it float in the wrong direction.

When the master's assistant awoke,
Beardie went back down to his main duty of
Rowing the oars with the ship's youngest boatswain,
Taking most of the weight of the water.

When a half-sleeping drunken sailor showed,
He went up and worked on the sloop's rigging,
Adjusting the stay rope that supported
The mainmast, tweaking the wires
And chains, mending holes in the sails,
That had of late started missing the wind.

Then he opened a barrel of meat
And carried a bowl of it to the kitchen,
Where the cook was waiting for him.

Suddenly, the captain shouted, "Prey!"
So Beardie ran below and loaded the cannon balls,
Lit the fuse, closing his ears before the "Boom!"
"Royal navy!" the captain yelled from the deck,
So Beardie extinguished the new fuse and sat
At the oars and rowed like the Devil until midnight,
When it was his shift to sleep and he rolled onto a hammock.

A Highland Legend

Shepherd Robert Stuart fell in love wi'
The saul o' the bonnie dochter Mary.
But her father objected to the match,
And cast Robin out as not weel-doing.

But when the father was away,
The couple met in secret for a walk
And a meal in the blooming forest.

In a passion, Robin declared that he wauld
Eve' be happy wi' living wi' her aun a
Tiny floating witch's islet in the middle o' the loch.
Mary took him up aun it and stepped
Aunto the islet, but the Hielandman
Jumped aun wi' too much force
And it floated briskly to the middle of the lake.

Many hours passed and the islet
Started sinking, but stopped
Short of the couple drowning.
Night came and they heard
Ghosts wailing around them.
The water crept up at night,
And their feet started freezing,
So Robin decided to pray to the Lord.

Their prayers were answered
When the moon came out and
They figured out that gif they
Raised the plaid, they were usin'
As a cover from the cold, it acted as a sail.
And the islet started moving towards the shore.

Ere they moored, they saw
Mary's father aun the bay.
They hid, but then came out
But didn't see the father.
Meantime, the father went into the
Water aun a different part
Of the loch, trying to save them.

He spent the night in the lake,
Searching for his chield,
And when he came back home,
He exclaimed upon seeing them alive,
"Aweel, Aweel," and agreed that Robin
Was a gudeman and that surely
They were meant to be married.

Note: Based on Sir Thomas Dick Lauder's 1880 "The Floating Islet," from *Highland Legends*.

Vestri's Confession

In the times of the Thirty Years War,
Germany was torn into two camps,
One Protestant, one Catholic,
And belonging to the wrong
Sect could have meant death.

A party of zealots stumbled onto a
Shabby hut, no taller than four-feet
In an isolated part of the forest.
They barged in and found a dwarf.

"I-I-I-I'mmmm not a Catholicccc, no, no, no…"
They raised their fists to him, and he exclaimed,
"I'lll ha-ha-have you you know… I shhhhhaped
"The first human from mud with my my hands!"

The Catholics were stunned and looked around.
There were statues, fine art and gold jewelry on the walls.
"I don't want want want nothin' from you, leave me be.
"The g-g-gods gave gave that mmmmmmold life!"

"He's just a crazy old, unfortunate man," an elderly said.
The others shrugged and left him alone.
As they exited, Vestri became enraged and started a
Whirlwind that spread destruction to many and ended the War.

PART III

WORK AND ART

Managing a Porn Star

When I couldn't sell my screenplays in Los Angeles,
I decided to try becoming a talent manager.
My first client was an internationally-known porn star.
She invited me to her pent-house studio for the interview.

It was then that I realized that she thought that I was joking,
Thinking that my true dream was becoming a porn star myself…
It was an awkward moment as I explained that I did not want to
Tour the bedroom, where they were preparing for a new shoot.

I took out my notepad and pen and asked her how I might help her.
She took a second look at my old suit and bun and took out
Her book, called, *True Sex*, with her nude on the cover.
I was relieved and looked through the contents.

She needed a press release to help sell the book, as there were
Few reviews… I didn't dare explain that it's not that kind of genre…
So, we talked about her wanting to become a film star,
And discussed doing comedy shows first.

She told me about her early traumatic sexual experiences.
And I asked her if she felt comfortable sharing them in public…
And then she giggled, and poked me painfully in the nose.
"That was very rude!" I exclaimed and jumped up.
"Sorry," she apologized. That ended my management of a porn star.

Rock Star's Double

On a warm night in Boston, I interviewed a rock star's double.
He was a classic, from the days of Elvis and the Beatles.
He crouched with crossed knees on the stage
And hummed and sang, like the audience was his kin-folk.
His wig was wild and thick, and we stared at it in awe.
I read his autobiography before coming, about all the
Famous celebrities that he met, and about all the lovers he had.
And now he was singing ballads, and cooed sixties flower-music.
His sonorous tone put me into a trance and I felt my head nodding.
Suddenly, he stopped and the audience moved to the door in a sea.
I went up to the manager and asked if I might interview the star.
I was told to wait outside the back door, in case he came out.
It was a piece for the *Cambridge Chronicle*… a major metro paper…
Still, it was warm, and I waited outside in a crowd of fans for an hour.
A short, thin, bold man, with a hoarse voice exited and gave a slow run.
The crowd followed him for a bit, and so did I.
"But, who are you?" I asked his back.
"I'm him of course." "But if you are him, who's you?"

Reading Poetry at Open-Mic Night in Columbia

Poetry is frequently a lonely craft, done on a wooden desk.
But, unlike wine, it grows stale when it ferments without fresh air.
The bar, where the open-mics were held smelled of beer and cigars,
But on its floor, kids and old men created art, not with their words,
But with their acts, with the booming yell, and the low sighs,
By dancing as they sang serenades of love coming and going as a tide.
Some wore tall hats, and others rimmed glasses.
Some wore make up, and others brought their wives and lasses.
And the audience was the most entertaining part of the show,
The old boys at the bar fainting from drink, laughing out of tune,
The young girls fluttering their lashes at the cavaliers of the stage,
The bartender yelling for orders, and the waitress demanding a bill.
 There is no better cure for an indecisive pen
Than scribbling as your neighbor suddenly droops, and goes to bed.

The Heckler: Or, Stand-Up Comedy

The lights are off, with only dim candles flickering on the tables.
You listen to a dozen obscene rants about sex, drugs and dogs,
Until your name is called and you grab your notes, and
Stumble over outstretched feet, and mount the two-foot stage.
You start to tell a tale about the time you visited the Oval Office…
"You're crazy!" a heckler screams from the front row.
You try to ignore him, and describe the slight mistake you made…
"Get off the stage!" he screams again, his pupils dilated.
You glance over at the headhunter at the front, grinning,
And you scream back a joke or two at the heckler,
And the headhunter stops grinning because you are a lady,
And ladies don't talk back.

To Tell a Poem

Ice tumbles in the shaker.
A girl whispers "whiskey" at the bar.
Footsteps stop at the door,
Creek into the hall,
"Are you using this chair?"
Drags it to another table.
Now she's chairful.
You look around at watercolors,
At three, yes, Three guitars on stage,
At the feather in John's hat,
Twist your tongue into a straw,
Suck a beer bottle with contempt,
Suck a cigarette in one breath,
Go into the dark hall and
Scratch your dry winter skin,
Finger and separate your hair,
Inhale Others…
I'm reading up at the carpet,
Paper trembling in my hand.
They are all waiting to speak.

Improvisational Arguments

The Wolf proclaimed his right to eat.
Little Red Hood objected to being eaten.
Grandma yelled that she was wrongly eaten.
And a vegetarian was appalled by it all.
The class voted that the Wolf shouldn't
Eat meat, and declared him a grass-eater.
But the Wolff protested by eating them all.

Communal Script Writing

I asked the class to write plots for scripts at home,
And they returned with notes on how it should be told.
I then declared that we only had enough board space
To write a single script, and couldn't fit them all.

I called for hands to vote on how the story would unfold.
One student wanted the hero to be a witch, another cowboy.
One wanted a tail, another hat, another sword.
The girls demanded heroines, the boys, heroes.

I added all to the script, and drew a plot on the board.
The cowboy witch he-she was fighting with
A gang of gnomes, mermaids, hunters and fairies,
And in the end he-she both won and lost.

The Slush Pile

Running a press means digging through the slush pile.
A slush pile is infrequently muddy, or stained.
But it is tall and wide, and always grows like the teeth
That when spread across a field, bloom into soldiers.

Two hundred submissions one month, then a thousand.
At first you promise to read every word of the book,
Then the first pages, then the first words, then scan,
As you work to keep up with your own deadlines.

And when you ask writers if you can edit their work,
But they reply that it is edited, and that they won't let you,
You know this means the pile will go down that day,
And you plow through it, and it's your job for it to never end.

PART IV

POLITICS

Campaigning for the Presidency

I was in New Hampshire on the campaign trail.
I shook hands and handed out fliers to dozens of voters,
Who all said that they see the campaign train
Roll by every four years, and that they were tired of the noise.

How can a Senator shake a million hands?
Why, with the help of thousands of volunteers,
Who might all hope for a job in the White House,
But it's a small House, and it's barely white.

So, the troops read the same tired message
By phone and in person to thousands of people,
Who are politically apathetical because of this process,
And stay home on Election Day to avoid the long lines.

And the Presidential hopeful goes on shows,
And plays guitar and does a dance once a month
To cheer the troops to shake-shake-shake,
While a few new interns cry in the back.

A Petition for Online Voting

We have all heard of the problems with electronic ballots;
Still, we are forced to vote electronically in rigged elections.
So, I would like to petition for online voting.
If ninety percent of the country has access to the web,
We can all allocate five minutes to log on and vote.
Who can tolerate the insults, shoving and hubbub
At the poll booths on Election Day, as we are given eight hours
To drop our jobs, and wait to vote in a ballot that will be discounted.
Why would poor people vote for wealthy business men?
Why can't somebody rise up with the compassion for true change
Not electoral change, but national change for the better?
We cannot see a fair election until workaholics,
Who eat lunch at their desks, are allowed to vote.
We will only have a true democracy when the vote is free.

Revolution

Marshall Charlie put his gun downwind to the Eagle Spring.
He shot a hundred gray buffalo with spread-out horns in that first hour.
But, that night the Spring rose up, and flooded, and rotted them.
Uncle got more to skin, to peg, to dry, to stack,
Until their carcasses salted the Great Spring, just for their tongues.

Their babes were left to starve, just for their tongues,
For Martha to feast on a boiled and spiced tongue.
Listen to the wounded wailing, to the faint heartbeat of my moccasins.
They are lined with free-roaming, bleached, freighted fertilizer-bones

That the Great Spirit stole in the night, when the white man
Was counting his green plants, listening to the train's engine—
Revola-la-la-la-lution.

A Jacobite Rebellion

Once upon a time, England fired King James,
Who fled to Scotland and incited rebellions,
Claiming that the crown was rightfully his,
And that it was withdrawn for his religion.

King James lost, but he had children and they
Fought for the rights of their dynasty with
The help of the ferocious Highlanders in kilts.
Sometimes, they marched in victory over English armies.

Until, one day, the Jacobites were not fighting
For King James's children, but for the Scottish
Nation, and for their kilts, and for the Scots tongue,
And they bled for their land and freedom and lost.

And their loss was tragic because they fought
Justly for a cause that was their inherent right.
They are called the Jacobite rebellions
Because they lost, and did not revolve the system.

Do We Need a President?

Does anybody have proof that the President
Does something besides swimming, when
He is not on the camera, giving interviews?
Does he calculate what might help the country
Recover from over a decade of recessions?
Or does he calculate what will line his pockets?
Can the country look, with a candid camera,
Into the Oval Office to find out what he does
On an average day? Does he read every brief
That comes before the Senate, or the Supreme Court?
When he visits foreign countries, does
He speak with foreign dignitaries, or tour the country?
Does he take credit for the work his interns do?
Why does he have a staff of thousands?
What do they do, if phone calls and letters
Remain un-answered, and problems are unsolved?
If we had four years without a president,
Would we notice any difference, besides the
Absence of the "final word" on issues,
And no single man to send millions to War?

Debt Ceiling

America hit the debt ceiling,
And kept spending money
Building fancy new colleges,
Bailing out car companies,
Banks, foreign countries,
Home owners and other
Wealthy groups, keeping
The minimum wage stable,
Not increasing welfare benefits,
And failing to help those starving,
Homeless, isolated, unrepresented.
Yet, unlike with the Soviet Union,
No state proposes to separate,
Even states that are conservative
And have savings, stay in the U.S.
Will we see out-migration to Mexico?
Will this country collapse
Because there was nobody sane
Or logical to take the reins and
Steer the Giant out of the debt-trap?

The Queen Visits Ireland

For the first time in over a hundred years,
The Queen visited Ireland this spring,
On the anniversary of the Dublin and Monaghan
Bombings of Irish nationalists, for which the
Perpetrators were not prosecuted.
George the Fifth visited exactly
A hundred years earlier, and even then
The nationalists saw British troops
And the union with England
As an occupation of the Irish Republic.
The Queen is the Commander in Chief
Of the British Army, and not a figurehead.
Irish referendums and polls show
A majority stands against the union.
Yet, millions are spent on the Queen's visit.
There are reports of two attempted bombings
On the Queen and her entourage.
But they are stopped and the visit ends.
Why did the Queen visit Ireland this spring?

Billion Dollar Thefts of Iraqi Funds

In the largest robbery in world history,
A billion was carted out in trucks from the
Central Bank of Iraq. But this is a penny
Compared with the twelve billion that was
Flown in a cargo plane by Pentagon officials
And disappeared from account books
Into the pockets of officials and contractors.
But these thefts are still a fraction of the
Nine-hundred billion that the War cost,
Or the three trillion that it robbed from the U.S.
Economy, which has remained in a recession.
World War II did not take us out of the Depression.
The unemployment rate dropped from
Twenty percent long before the War started.
But, today with computers to estimate
The potential economic impact, we went
To war at the worst time, without just cause,
And meanwhile trillions of dollars were stolen.
Every tax-paying American should be invested
In putting the perpetrators on trial,
So we might recuperate our lost earnings.

The First Decade of the Iraq War

From one to six hundred thousand Iraqis died
Violently in the first eight years of the Iraq War.
President Barack Obama announced plans to
End the War a year ago, in an early speech.
Now he is pushing withdrawal from Afghanistan
Back to three years from now, perhaps once
He is no longer a president, and others are in charge.
The election slogan on his website is, "Are you in?"
As if he is running in a prom queen contest.
I'm not "in" support of killing any more Iraqis
Without any further attacks on the US soil,
With a comparatively low death-rate of US soldiers,
And with a functioning Iraqi government in place.
Anti-war protests stopped the year Obama took office
Because he promised to withdraw long ago.
Even if there were protests in DC, I would not march
Outside the windows of the White House,
While the staff eats chocolate truffles and lobsters.
I would not walk in a crowd, screaming
Somebody else's slogans in the heat or rain.
But, I will write these political poems to exclaim
That I object to irrational and inhumane policies.

Mandatory Execution of Gang Members

Obama voted against a bill
For the mandatory execution
Of gang members who kill cops.
But I think this is a swell idea.
What if there was a law for
The mandatory execution
Of all gang members who kill?
Why should cops have
Special treatment under the law?
What about an innocent child
Killed by a gangster's hand?
Why send a gangster to prison,
Where he could run a prison gang?
Those who support gun-ownership,
Should also support the mandatory
Executions of all violent gang members.

Taxes

I paid over twenty thousand dollars in taxes this year.
I was homeless on welfare on five thousand per year.
Now I drive to work on cracked and unfixed roads.
When I email my senators and congressmen for help,
They don't reply, or send automated messages.
It's tough finding a job as all states are cutting their
Higher education budgets, despite rising enrollments.
Electricity costs are over two-hundred dollars per month.
Hospitals have outdated equipment, and untrained staff.
The police and F.B.I. can't help when I appeal for help.
Are my tax dollars going to Iraq or into corrupt pockets?
Can I appeal for boycotting paying taxes until my requests
For assistance are met? Can I invest my money instead
In off-shore accounts, saving them in case the U.S. collapses?
Can I invest my money into helping myself if I need help?
Can I spend that money on my own private security guards?
What about my own private doctors and medical equipment?
Why can't people band together with their co-workers,
Not in unions, but in joint medical and security funds,
Where they would all know exactly where every penny
Of their savings is going, and that it is benefiting them?

Faculty Are Managers in Ohio

Ohio voted to call all faculty members "managers."
The rest of the country might want to follow.
It is a fact that faculty are on yearly contracts.
They are middle-management because only the Dean
Of their college has authority over their practices.
Only the President of the school can terminate them.
Faculty manage the students' behavior and attendance.
Faculty discipline, grade, judge, and evaluate.
Faculty are managers when they are teaching,
And manage when they create new classes.
My cheers to laws that recognize the role of the faculty.

An Online Education

I have never taken an online class.
But I am certified to teach online.
I wish I went to high school online.
Instead of dealing with the taunts,
Practical jokes, bullying et cetera,
Instead, I could have read Emily Dickenson,
And written A.P. English essays
From the comfort of my home.
I bet I would have scored better
On the S.A.T. if I had more study-time.
I would have published this book
By the time I graduated from school.
And instead of saying that I was
Home-schooled on college essays,
I would be able to say that I went
To a regular school listed on the transcript.
In over twenty years of my education,
Did I learn anything from my teachers?
Or did I learn it all from books and practice?
And if the latter, wouldn't we all
Benefit from an online education?
Just give kids free laptops and internet.

If I Had a Robot Assistant

If I had a robot assistant,
It would be shipped to a
Conference for me
With a recorded tape
Of my professional lecture.
It would give tests for me,
And I would watch from home,
Catching cheaters with my
Third eye in its metal-head.
Sometimes it would monitor
My classes as I lecture.
And it would tell students to stop
Using their cell phones,
When it would pick up on
The phones' texting waves.
Every professor should have one.

School vs. Town Elections

In all my years of complaining about the system,
I won only two elections: at UMass and in Town Hall.
At UMass, I won by promoting adding paper towels
To the dirty and barren college dorm bathrooms.
My roommate drew a wet-hands-shaking poster.
I shook hands with everybody in my building.
Winning in the Framingham Town Hall was easier.
I gave a speech for the Town Board, which was
Broadcast to every home in the region,
Explaining that I had an MA, and that there were
No other candidates competing for the job.
As the Senator, I was always in the minority,
And you can guess where I was as a
Representative of culture in a Boston suburb.
If I had to run again, I would pick a more
Competitive race, and would choose a county
Where my views would be in the majority.

No More Snow in Moscow

While Al Gore is worrying about global warming,
And tsunamis, hurricanes, and other disasters are on the rise,
The Muscovites have finally invented a cure-all.
They have started bombing clouds with a gas
That destroys snow in the winter over the Moscow skies.
Now, it appears that I left Moscow for America
To be stuck in snow storms in the PA mountains.
Americans used to do nuclear tests in the desert
That blew a hole through the ozone layer,
So the Russians are being modest as they
Simply divert the snow from the capital,
And double the snow-fall in the surrounding towns.

Graduate Student Unions

There are Graduate Students at NYU that make
As much as an entry-level clerk at the Metro.
But there are Graduate Students at smaller schools
That make as much as a welfare recipient.
Yet, N.Y.U. has a union, but public and regional
Graduate programs don't have grad unions.
So in some state universities, faculty unions
Keep faculty salaries high enough to out-do N.Y.U.,
But graduate salaries lower than the Mexican
Minimum wage, after taxes are subtracted.
Of course since many assistantships only
Last a year or two, by the time you strike,
You have graduated and joined the faculty union.

Why Is There a Monarchy in England?

Sixteen out of the world's forty-four monarchies
Recognize Queen Elizabeth the Second as their head.
Only the Pope's Vatican City has an absolute monarchy
In Europe; in the east, Saudi Arabia has an absolute ruler.
Power is still transferred on through hereditary lines in Spain.
But Spain does not rule over countries in nearly every continent.
Canada and Australia are both nearly as large as the U.S.
How can an elderly woman in London be the military
Commander of countries that barely have a language in common?
With all the fuss about the Middle Eastern revolutions,
And despite all the revolutions England suffered,
Can any political analyst explain how the Queen
Held onto power throughout the twentieth century?
I know that rich folks in America own large
Chunks of land, but what if Bill Gates owned the continent?
I'm not even sure if it's wrong, I just wish I knew how she does it.
I wish she would sign it over, so I could try it.

Why Is Gas the Popular Fuel?

Perhaps I snoozed in science class,
But why is gas the popular fuel?
Why not grass, or feces?
Why didn't anybody invent
Cheaper battery-only cars?
Why has it taken a century
For people to start considering
Alternative fuel options?
And if we have to stay with oil,
Why does old oil of rotten animals
Cost four dollars per gallon,
But milk still costs one dollar?
If it needs to be combustible,
Why don't they try loading
Regular kitchen oil into cars?
It's cheaper than gas per gallon.
If we have a universal education,
Shouldn't there be more inventions?
And if there are enough inventions,
What's stopping the production?

Deepwater Horizon

When the Deepwater Horizon rig exploded,
It killed eleven, and spilled two-hundred
Million gallons of BP oil into the Gulf Coast.
A year later, they will start drilling again,
While the marshes in Louisiana are still black,
And pelicans are brown and eat and drink oil.
The Gulf Coast also touches Cuba and Mexico.
It has some of the best tropical beaches
In America, and has many other resources.
And a single company, in one accident,
Put all those things at risk of closure.
I am not an environmentalist, but I think it is
Criminal to kill millions of fish, birds and plants,
And to destroy the value of Coast properties.
And yet, a year after the incident, no charges
Are filed, oil prices are up, and they'll keep drilling.

"Most Presidents Have Ignored the War Powers Act"

"Most Presidents have ignored the War Powers Act,"
McCain said about a possible invasion of Lybia.
We are already in Iraq and Afghanistan.
Does the President need to ask for permission
To declare war? Can any person send men to die
Without asking them and their families for permission?
If the President is not in the front lines of the fight;
Then, nobody will be, "taking shots at the President."
We are told it is pro-American to approve of the President's policy.
But is it pro-American to approve the policy of
Not asking for permission to declare war?
Is it American to bypass the democratic process,
And for the President to make tyrannical decisions?
"The only way Congress can act is to cut off funding,
"Which is what they did in the Vietnam war…
"They cannot command to the Commander in Chief…
"Would've been a whole lot easier a couple of months ago my friend…"
Would have been easier to make acts of war
Before the presidential election is at full-speed?
No President can justify ignoring the War Powers Act.

Should We Sing "Barney" during Shootings?

Rivera Alanis sang a Barney song about chocolate
During a shooting in a city in Mexico's financial hub.
She was teaching a kindergarten class when they
Heard the first shots, and they all dropped to the floor.
Rivera turned on her blackberry phone and recorded
A few of the kids screaming in fear, as the shots rang.
Five people were being executed by a drug cartel.
Then, the teacher has an epiphany and leads the kids
In a Barney song and their voices are joyous, as
They sing a familiar song, they must sing regularly.
That teacher was trained to encourage optimism
By the Security Commission program for teachers.

There is no similar program in America, but I wonder
What would have happened if I started singing Barney
When I worked as a substitute teacher for a
Juvenile correction facility in Los Angeles County
During a fight I witnessed in my class between
Two Mexican seventeen-year-old gangsters,
Who started hitting each other with fists,
And almost lifted a metal desk to help their blows.
Er… I just don't think it would have helped.
I called, "Security" and that stopped the fight.
But, I would like to see more evidence on the
Impact of Barney on violent conflicts…

How Much Does a Senate Seat Cost?

Dickens was frequently asked to run for office
But always declined, blaming corruption,
In other words, he couldn't afford buying the seat.
Many earlier British authors, like Disraeli in *Sybil*,
Publicized that seats were sold to highest bidders.
Activists campaigned for election reforms,
And representatives started to be paid for their work,
Instead of paying bribes to win the jobs.
But it seems that something has gone awry once more.
The F.B.I. found overwhelming evidence that
Blagojevich was asking for millions for the Chicago
Senate seat that was previously held by Obama.
But, years later, he was only found guilty on one
Out of twenty-five counts, and is appealing a
Miserly potential five-year prison sentence.
If it is legal to sell Senate seats, should those
Jobs just come with a price tag, like—five million?
Should folks who want to abide by the law be
Allowed to bid on these jobs, if that's how they are won?
As tempting as Blagojevich's book-deals and press are,
I just don't want to commit political suicide for them.
And, is the F.B.I. guilty of creating twenty-four
False, or completely unsubstantiated charges,
Or is the Judge on the case guilty of not finding
Overwhelming F.B.I. evidence enough for a conviction?
I hope he appeals this case to the Supreme Court
Because I would like to read their ruling on this one.

PART V

PETITIONS AGAINST MARRIAGE

A Borrowed Lover

He purrs when I give him a brownie to eat.
He licks my face, just above my mouth,
Spilling saliva, words, emotions,
Until this page is covered with mud
From my lover's dirty paws.
He bites my fingers.
Sits on my shoulders.
I throw him off my thighs.
He spreads his legs.
Licks himself.
Gets sluggish from the repetition.
A train blows.
He becomes a hairy ball,
Crouched in a fetus-position on my bed.
He belongs to my neighbor.
I'm borrowing him for the night.

He Looks Down

He lives in an abandoned, unfinished jail,
In a roofless watchtower with broken windows.
There is glass, beer cans, and dried ivy on the floor.
When he sleeps, little bugs get into his nose,
Big bugs sit on his unclothed hands,
Ladybugs crawl all over his walls,
Bees wake him up with a buzz in the morning.
He is allergic to bug-bites.
He is afraid of growing sick from dirt.
He stays because he needs a place of his own.
One day, rain starts.
It soaks his sheets and rags.
He runs out and hides under the bridge.
He sleeps on a wire coach that fishermen left.
Rain is falling on the river,
On cars, speeding over the bridge.
It pours heavily, like maternal fluids.
Then it stops.
And he walks over through a graffiti, abandoned bridge,
To his sewage-wrecked, abandoned jail,
Into his bug-infested tower,
And he hugs his knees.
And he wants a drink, a smoke, a caress.
But he is dirty and unshaven.
So, he stands up—
Too tired to remain seated.
And he looks down at the wall of the unfinished jail,

And down further at the trees and at the river far below.

And he climbs out of his window,
Cutting his hand on the broken glass.
And he walks along the wall,
And looks down at the sparkling clean water of the river.
And he looks down—

Confused Youth

1.

A youth of ecstatic escape—
Sloping into a white blanket,
Gripping a railing on a train
Under a table on *my* island.
Through construction pipes,
Running from their shouts,
From a camp to raspberries,
Into a faint from math class.

2.

A table isn't big enough; at ten,
Boys started throwing peas.
I delighted in reporting them
And hearing their pleas.
I skated to lakes to think.
I kissed skaters to feel,
Not to be bound with a ring,
Or to avoid a hefty bill.

3.

Beauty lies in freedom;
Freedom is an uphill road;
It don't care where you're from;
It lets amateurs row the boat;
It's sweetest in loneliness;
Gives riches in exile.

Katya

At a dead cypress lake,
Where trees stand stripped,
Gray in the still water,
She sits on the dock,
And looks into the distance,
To hide her swollen skin and tired eyes,
As a spoon of makeup slides down,
To her low-cut, silky dress,
And Geisha-Asian earrings
Of a divorced purchased-bride,
Waiting for his white cotton underwear,
With holes on both buttcheeks
That he'll hang on her closet's door,
Just below her x-husband's pictures,
Below the chapel of icons at the balcony,
In the garden of plants in her living room.

Wild Woman

She criticizes the oysters at a cocktail party.
She makes love on the floor of a club.
She reads a hand-bound book, inside the Dead Sea—
While others float with their heels up.
When it's time to kiss ass, she kicks it.
When she should cry, she shouts.
Inconsistency is her only consistence.
Her body is her temple of Basilica.
Hair that's falling from her crown is her scarf.
If you run with her she'll definitely eat you,
She will steal your thoughts and hopes.
But, then from your flexible bones—
She'll resurrect a newborn soul.
Now, she's flying somewhere between east and west.
Will you catch what Wild Woman says
Between hello and farewell?

The Resurrection of the Rose

It grew from lint when
I first touched your blouse.
Then with the gale of harsh words,
It withered and it died.
The flower turned from red to black,
And drooped its proud head.
I kept it in the vase,
Cutting a portion out.
As I cut you off,
And told you to desist,
Your love drew water afresh,
And sprung new leaves
Of green, unsoiled friendship.
But then you stopped your growth.
"'Tis all I got."
Now that my eyes no longer ache from tears,
I'll never ask a man
To buy a rose for me again.

I Need a Man

I need a man like I need glue
To stick my hand onto the dew.
Then, I'd own that nebulous nectar
Like the telescope owns a star.
That far-seer of stars is luckier—
They come back every night.
But my drops quickly expire
Till only glue is left to quit.

Can I Go Upstairs to the Girls' Apartment?

My suitor wore a hat and tie
And took me to the orchestra.
But when I didn't answer his
Tight embrace with equal strength,
He asked if I wouldn't mind
"Can I go up to the girls' apartment?"
I said, "Of course, you may."
And to my delight, he went up,
And stayed the night.

The Wind

Manipulation is like a gust of wind.
At first there is a draft, when he says,
"My family owns half of Charleston."
Then, the draft goes up and down,
As he withdraws, and then pursues,
Then, you feel an inflow into your loins,
And you can feel him stir within.
Just when you are lulled, you are suspended
Up on a mountain, and your car
Skids off to the side of the highway
As the mountain wind casts it to flight.
If you open your eyes and study the story,
You see the fool that you have been,
So you drive to lower ground,
And leave the crook in the nook with the wind.

Massage

In Latin *massa* means dough,
So, hands dig into the skin like
It's a pastry, being prepared.
Only it's made with muscle,
Skin and joints, so it's tough,
And the masseur pushes your
Back into the table and rotates
Your knots, and pours oil
To make the dough smoother,
And tanning lotion for color,
And scented perfume for smell,
And hot stones to cook the meal.

An Argument for the Illegalization of Marriage

Many argue for the legalization of gay marriage,
But few have considered a different campaign.
What about making marriage illegal for all?
Marriage does far more harm than good in practice.

A marriage is a contract that gives the husband
Rights to incarcerate the wife in a mental institution,
And to insist against intercourse with other males,
And to only give the food and clothing he desires.

Under a marriage contract, what rights does she have?
Can a wife insist on him staying for the children?
Will she receive more than the welfare rate if he leaves?
Will she ever recover her health or an education?

So, I would like to make an appeal against marriage,
And for life that is free of sexual and personal contracts.

The Guy with No Car

It's tough dating the guy with no car.
You have to drive two hours to
Pick him up and drop him home for
A weekend of him playing video games,
And you doing your research,
And him leaving to play games with others,
And you staying and working
On a poem about the guy
Without a car.

Skater after the Crash

What do popular skaters do
After they crash on a jump?
Can they afford surgery?
What if they are left with
A limp, and can't skate again?
Do they move to the ocean
To park cars and sell tickets?
Do they spend money on
Alcohol, clubs and drugs?
Do they find pretty girls,
And use them for their money?
Do they steal, sell illegal stuff?
At thirty, I've stopped caring.

The Guy Who Stares

Have you met that guy who keeps
Staring at you as you walk by?
In the movies, this suggests attraction.
But, if you try saying, "Hello,"
He doesn't reply, and rushes away.
If you glance at him, his eyes drop.
If you wave, he runs away.
But whenever you are busy with
Your life, running down the hall,
He stares at you with his black eyes,
Blank, without a smile, or a grimace,
Just staring at your face, or
At your thighs, or chest, or…
You see him with other girls,
And holding hands with boys,
And he doesn't stare at them,
But he just can't stop staring at you…

Politics and Love

Once, I started a Russian Club
With a group of ten students.
I wrote the constitution,
The bylaws, and the grants.
I searched for the members,
Scheduled rooms and meetings,
Found Russian university presidents
To give talks at UMass for the group.
Then, I had a brisk tete-a-tete
With the Vice President and
The next day he joined with
The Secretary and staged a coup,
And suddenly I was out of the club.

Prom with M.I.T.

I could only afford a twenty-dollar dress to the prom.
But I had to go by limousine because my date was rich.
I asked him out because he was accepted to M.I.T.
I met him on the street littered with mansions in my old shoes.
He was dressed in an Armani suite, with a butterfly.
The other girls wore tiaras and flowers on their wrists.
His friends were going to Stanford and Harvard,
So they kept teasing him for M.I.T.'s high suicide rate.
We only had a couple of dances, everybody wanted him.
We returned to the mansion late at night and
I started to suspect that the rest of the guys brought
Ladies of the night, as a bit of an orgy sailed off.
And just when my date winked at me, and stood close,
I asked him to drive me home, and never dated M.I.T. again.

The Last Kiss

I gave him a massage with scented cream,
And we fit like two parts of a seashell.
But suddenly, after a kiss, he started chanting,
And he screamed and raged, until I went
Up to the top bunk and tried to fall asleep.
But he kept screaming and picked up a knife,
So I climbed down and asked him to stop,
But he raised it high and cut the back of my hand.
I ran outside and cried bitterly with grief,
Then returned and asked him to leave.
But he put the knife to his wrists
And slid them three times on each.
I called the cops and he went into rehab.
I nursed him to health and in return
He stole my money and abused me.
It's been six years, and that was my last kiss.

Captured Grasshopper

Your breath once touched this glass,
A mist on a crystal mountain,
Now a prison for a grasshopper.
Drops turn my skin from dirt to mud.
I grab my white, dimpled right breast.
Thoughts pound there—like a child.
I'm used to my tile-hopping babe.
It hops, and stretches, and scratches
And stares up with beady eyes.
My sponge used to fly like a dagger.
Shampoo had a second to touch my roots.
I jumped out, higher than him,
"What if it jumps on my ars!"
Now he's in your glass.
I can suffocate him,
Drown him,
Abandon him,
Banish him.
I breathe.
I let the soft drops kiss my lips.
The grasshopper waits.

Spring and Beauty

On a utopian island with my daimon
Under the red straws of a broken hat
With Huxley and Adorno in my bag.
A humming bird beats on the fountain.
I'm feasting on a sweat-flavored duck,
With my feet in knitted black stockings
Up on a table I painted with angels,
Vulnerable purple flowers and ivy
Branches erupting with innocent leaves.
I used to yearn for romance
But after you I only yearn for peace.
Don't approach!
I have a restraining-order on you.
You detached me from myself.
Now you can't approach!
Because I'm remembering myself.

Associations

I think of you when I smell cigar smoke,
When I'm at a pond with stagnant water,
When I sit at my desk with an opened window,
And smell the strong odor of the freshly mowed lawn,
When cars stop in front of me abruptly,
And I hit the brakes, and smell tires burning,
When my neighbor burns his hay in a rusted bucket,
When I scratch a pimple and the blood dries,
Before I clean my room, when it's dusty, and mildewed,
When my landlord paints the hall and keeps doors closed.
I think of you, and I'm glad I'm alone.

Fomite
Burlington, Vermont

Fomite is a literary press whose authors and artists explore the human condition -- political, cultural, personal and historical -- in poetry and prose.

A fomite is a medium capable of transmitting infectious organisms from one individual to another.

Loisaida
by Dan Chodorokoff

Catherine, a young anarchist estranged from her parents and squatting in an abandoned building on New York's Lower East Side is fighting with her boyfriend and conflicted about her work on an underground newspaper. After learning of a developer's plans to demolish a community garden, Catherine builds an alliance with a group of Puerto Rican community activists. Together they confront the confluence of politics, money, and real estate that rule Manhattan. All the while she learns important lessons from her great-grandmother's life in the Yiddish anarchist movement that flourished on the Lower East Side at the turn of the century. In this coming of age story, family saga, and tale of urban politics, Dan Chodorkoff explores the "principle of hope", and examines how memory and imagination inform social change.

℘ ℘ ℘

When You Remember Deir Yassin
by R.L Green

When You Remember Deir Yassin is a collection of poems by R. L. Green, an American Jewish writer, on the subject of the occupation and destruction of Palestine. Green comments: "Outspoken Jewish critics of Israeli crimes against humanity have, strangely, been called "anti-Semitic" and as well as the hilariously illogical epithet "self-hating Jews." As a Jewish critic of the Israeli government, I have come to accept it these accusations as a stamp of approval and a badge of honor, signifying my own fealty to a central element of Jewish identity and ethics: one must be a lover of truth and a friend to the oppressed, and stand with the victims of tyranny, not with the tyrants, despite tribal loyalty or self-advancement. These poems were written as expressions of outrage, and of grief, and to encourage my sisters and brothers of every cultural or national grouping to speak out against injustice, to try to save Pal - estine, and in so doing, to reclaim for myself my own place as part of the

Fomite
Burlington, Vermont

The Co-Conspirator's Tale

by Ron Jacobs

There's a place where love and mistrust are never at peace; where duplicity and deceit are the universal currency. *The Co-Conspirator's Tale* takes place within this nebulous firmament. There are crimes committed by the police in the name of the law. Excess in the name of revolution. The combination leaves death in its wake and the survivors struggling to find justice in a San Francisco Bay Area noir by the author of the underground classic *The Way the Wind Blew:A History of the Weather Underground* and the novel *Short Order Frame Up*.

Kasper Planet: Comix and Tragix

by Peter Schumann

Kasper from Persian **G**hendsh-Bar carrier of **treasures** What treasures Treasures of junk Degrader of the **Precious**ness system Also from India Vidushaka Also medieval subversive thrown out **of** cathedral into marketplace A midget speaking swazzel language which **cops** don't speak

Fomite
Burlington, Vermont

Views Cost Extra
by L.E. Smith

Views that inspire, that calm, or that terrify – all come at some cost to the viewer. In *Views Cost Extra* you will find a New Jersey high school preppy who wants to inhabit the "perfect" cowboy movie, a rural mailman disgusted with the residents of his town who wants to live with the penguins, an ailing screen writer who strikes a deal with Johnny Cash to reverse an old man's failures, an old man who ponders a young man's suicide attempt, a one-armed blind blues singer who wants to reunite with the car that took her arm on the assembly line -- and more. These stories suggest that we must pay something to live even ordinary lives.

✄ ✄ ✄

The Empty Notebook Interrogates Itself
by Susan Thomas

The Empty Notebook began its life as a very literal metaphor for a few weeks of what the poet thought was writer's block, but was really the struggle of an eccentric persona to take over her working life. It won. And for the next three years everything she wrote came to her in the voice of the Empty Notebook, who, as the notebook began to fill itself, became rather opinionated, changed gender, alternately acted as bully and victim, had many bizarre adventures in exotic locales and developed a somewhat politically-incorrect attitude. It then began to steal the voices and forms of other poets and tried to immortalize itself in various poetry reviews. It is now thrilled to collect itself in one slim volume

✄ ✄ ✄

Fomite

Burlington, Vermont

My God, What Have We Done?
by Susan Weiss
a world afflicted with war, toxicity, and hunger, does what we do in our private lives really matter? Fifty years after the creation of the atomic bomb at Los Alamos, newlyweds Pauline and Clifford visit that once-secret city on their honeymoon, compelled by Pauline's fascination with Oppenheimer, the soulful scientist. The two stories emerging from this visit reverberate back and forth between the loneliness of a new mother at home in Boston and the isolation of an entire community dedicated to the development of the bomb. While Pauline struggles with unforeseen challenges of family life, Oppenheimer and his crew reckon with forces beyond all imagining.

Finally the years of frantic research on the bomb culminate in a stunning test explosion that echoes a rupture in the couple's marriage. Against the backdrop of a civilization that's out of control, Pauline begins to understand the complex, potentially explosive physics of personal relationships.

At once funny and dead serious, *My God, What Have We Done?* sifts through the ruins left by the bomb in search of a more worthy human achievement.

※ ※ ※

"The activity of art is based on the capacity of people to be infected by the feelings of others." Tolstoy, *What is Art?*

www.ingramcontent.com/pod-product-compliance
Lightning Source LLC
Chambersburg PA
CBHW031253290426
44109CB00012B/560